Pumpkin Carving Tips

ALWAYS CARVE THE SMALLEST DETAILS 1ST, SAVING THE LARGEST GRAY AREAS FOR LAST!

WHEN CARVING THE LID, INSERT THE KNIFE AT AN ANGLE SO THE LID WON'T FALL THROUGH THE HOLE.

HAVE SOME NEWSPAPER WHERE YOU CAN PLACE THE DISCARDED PULP.

USE A METAL SPOON OR OTHER TOOL TO SCRAPE OFF THE STRINGS AND SEEDS, AND THIN THE SHELL OF THE PUMPKIN FOR EASIER CARVING.

PREVENT MOLD BY SPRAYING PUMPKIN WITH A MIXTURE OF WATER WITH A SMALL AMOUNT OF BLEACH.

HAPPY CARVING!

Instructions

METHOD 1

1. TAPE THE STENCIL TO THE PUMPKIN.

2. USE THE KNIFE CARVING TOOL TO CUT OUT GRAY SHAPES THROUGH THE PAPER.

3. ONCE FINISHED, REMOVE THE PAPER AND TAPE FROM PUMPKIN AND INSERT TEA CANDLE.

METHOD 2

1. TAPE THE STENCIL TO THE PUMPKIN.

2. USE A SHARP, POINTED TOOL TO PUNCH THROUGH THE PAPER, CREATING A DOTTED OUTLINE OF THE GRAY SHAPES

3. REMOVE PAPER AND CONNECT THE DOTS TO CARVE THE DESIGN INTO THE PUMPKIN.

HAPPY CARVING!

KSG
Press

KSG
Press

KSG
Press

KSG
Press

© KSG 2022. All Rights Reserved.

KSG
Press

KSG
Press

KSG
Press

KSG Press

KSG
Press

KSG
Press

KSG Press

KSG
Press

KSG
Press

1

KSG
Press

KSG
Press

KSG
Press

Made in the USA
Columbia, SC
12 October 2024

44131536R00030